SMASH POP HITS

Project Manager: Carol Cuellar
Cover Design: Martha L. Ramirez

CONTENTS

(GOD MUST HAVE SPENT)
A LITTLE MORE TIME ON YOU

Words and Music by
CARL STURKEN and EVAN ROGERS

Moderately slow

ALL STAR

Words and Music by
GREG CAMP

AMAZED

Words and Music by
MARV GREEN, AIMEE MAYO
and CHRIS LINDSEY

Slowly

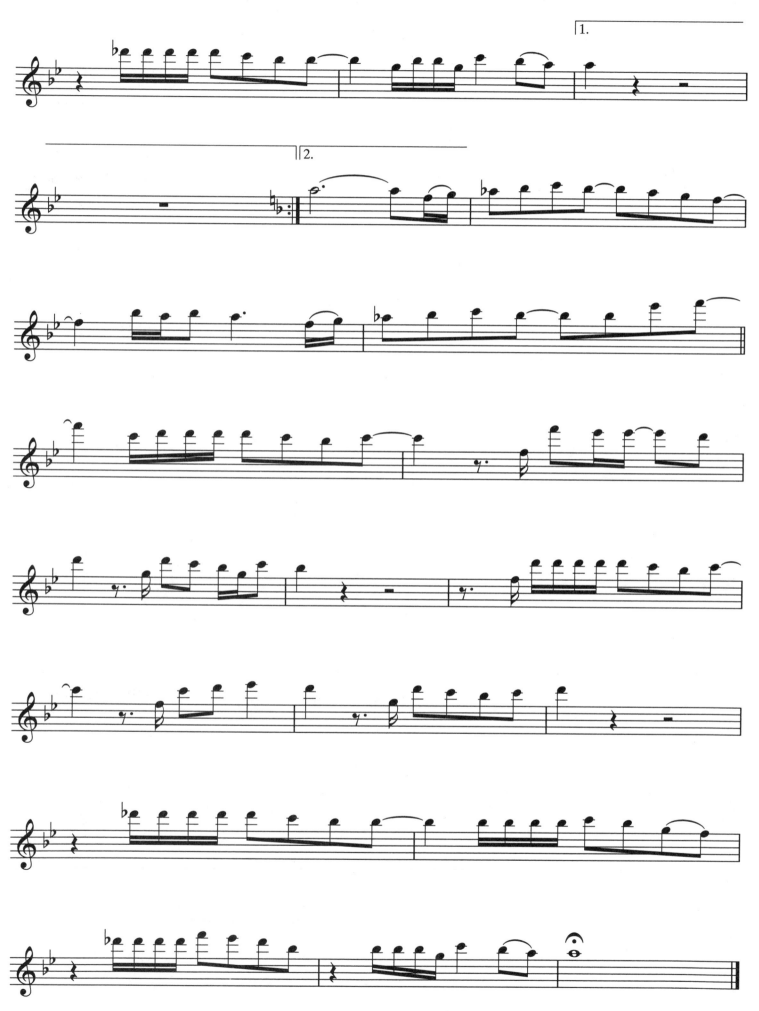

ANAKIN'S THEME

By JOHN WILLIAMS

AS LONG AS YOU LOVE ME

By MAX MARTIN

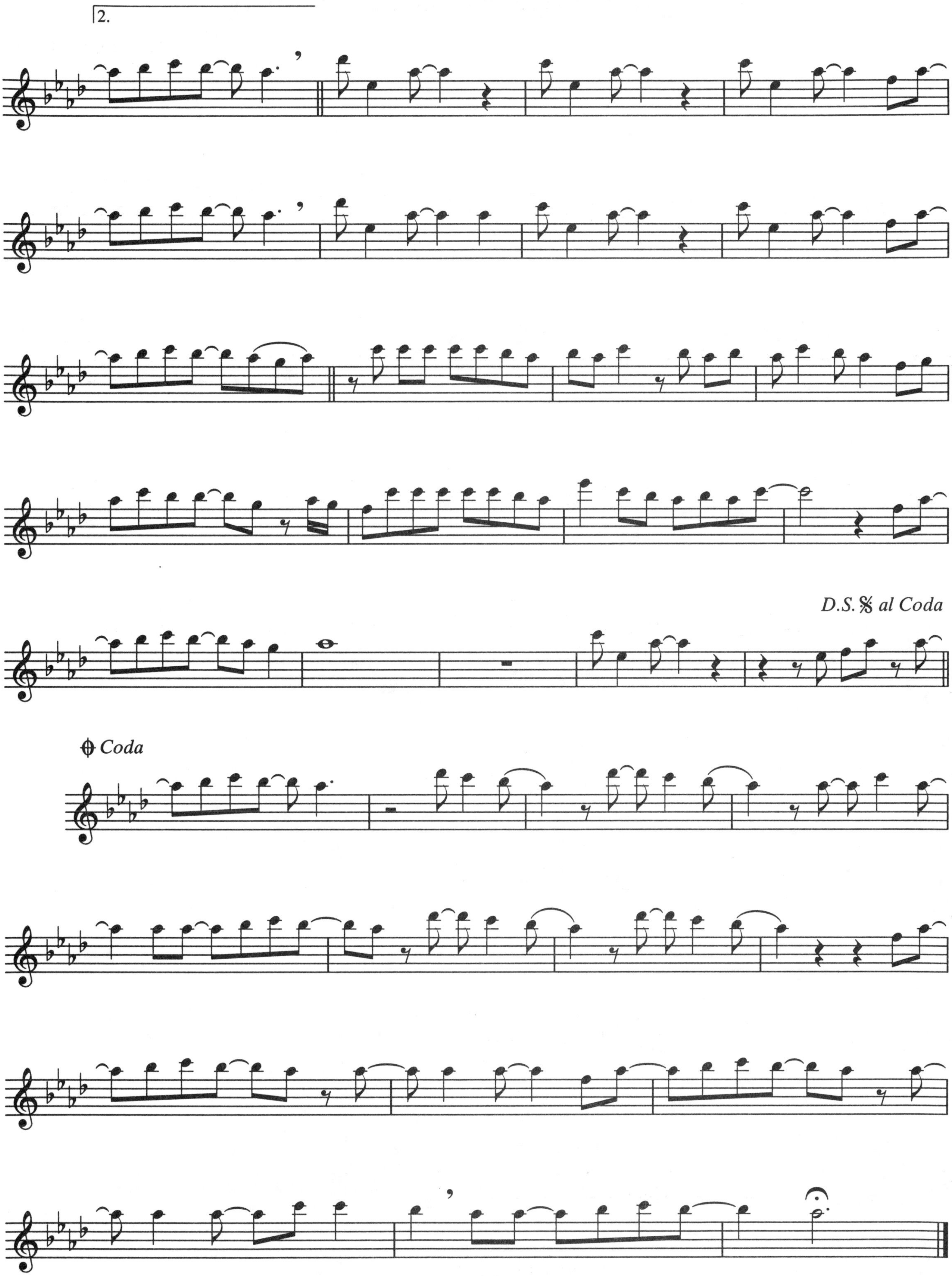
2.
D.S. 𝄋 al Coda
𝄌 Coda

...BABY ONE MORE TIME

Words and Music by
MAX MARTIN

Moderately (♩ = 96)

... Baby One More Time - 2 - 1
IF9939

BACK AT ONE

Words and Music by
BRIAN McKNIGHT

Back At One - 2 - 1
IF9939

rit.

BAILAMOS

Words and Music by
PAUL BARRY and MARK TAYLOR

rit.

BEAUTIFUL STRANGER

Words and Music by
MADONNA CICCONE and WILLIAM ORBIT

Beautiful Stranger - 2 - 1
IF9939

BELIEVE

Words and Music by
BRIAN HIGGINS, STUART McLENNAN, PAUL BARRY,
STEPHEN TORCH, MATT GRAY and TIM POWELL

Moderate disco beat

Believe - 2 - 1
IF9939

(YOU DRIVE ME) CRAZY

Words and Music by
JÖRGEN ELOFSSON, DAVID KREUGER,
PER MAGNUSSON and MAX MARTIN

Moderately slow

THE CUP OF LIFE

Words and Music by
ROBI ROSA, LUIS G. ESCOLAR
and DESMOND CHILD

25

DUEL OF THE FATES

By JOHN WILLIAMS

Duel of the Fates - 3 - 2
IF9939

I DO (CHERISH YOU)

Words and Music by
KEITH STEGALL and DAN HILL

IF9939

FROM THIS MOMENT ON

Words and Music by
SHANIA TWAIN and R.J. LANGE

Slowly (♩ = 72)

From This Moment On - 2 - 1
IF9939

GENIE IN A BOTTLE

Words and Music by
PAMELA SHEYNE, DAVID FRANK
and STEVE KIPNER

To Coda ⊕

Genie In a Bottle - 2 - 1
IF9939

I DON'T WANT TO MISS A THING

Words and Music by
DIANE WARREN

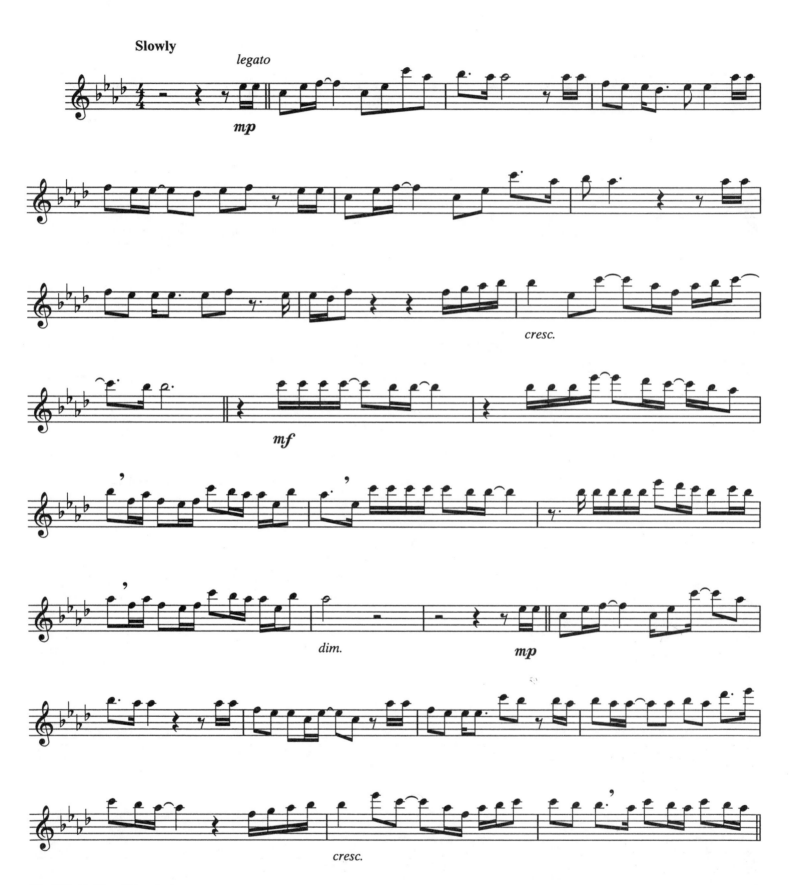

I Don't Want to Miss a Thing - 2 - 1
IF9939

I WANT IT THAT WAY

Words and Music by
MAX MARTIN and ANDREAS CARLSSON

rit.

I KNEW I LOVED YOU

Words and Music by
DARREN HAYES and DANIEL JONES

Moderately slow

I WILL REMEMBER YOU

Words and Music by
SEAMUS EGAN, SARAH McLACHLAN
and DAVE MERENDA

Moderately slow

mp

rit.

I'LL NEVER BREAK YOUR HEART

Words and Music by
ALBERT MANNO and EUGENE WILDE

Slowly

LOST IN YOU

Words and Music by
**WAYNE KIRKPATRICK, TOMMY SIMS
and GORDON KENNEDY**

IF I COULD TURN BACK
THE HANDS OF TIME

Words and Music by
R. KELLY

Moderately slow

If I Could Turn Back The Hands of Time - 2 - 1
IF9939

LARGER THAN LIFE

Words and Music by
MAX MARTIN, KRISTIAN LUNDIN
and BRIAN T. LITTRELL

Medium rock

Larger Than Life - 2 - 1
IF9939

LIVIN' LA VIDA LOCA

Words and Music by
ROBI ROSA and DESMOND CHILD

Fast (♩ = 138)

MAN! I FEEL LIKE A WOMAN!

Words and Music by
SHANIA TWAIN and R.J. LANGE

Moderate shuffle rock (♩ = 120)

Man! I Feel Like a Woman! - 2 - 1
IF9939

MUSIC OF MY HEART

Words and Music by
DIANE WARREN

NOTHING REALLY MATTERS

Words and Music by
MADONNA CICCONE and PATRICK LEONARD

Moderately

Nothing Really Matters - 2 - 1
IF9939

STRONG ENOUGH

Words and Music by
MARK TAYLOR and PAUL BARRY

Moderate dance

Strong Enough - 3 - 1
IF9939

56

THE PRAYER

Words and Music by
CAROLE BAYER SAGER and DAVID FOSTER
Italian Lyric by ALBERTO TESTA and TONY RENIS

Slowly, with expression

SHAKE YOUR BON-BON

Words and Music by
ROBI ROSA, GEORGE NORIEGA
and DESMOND CHILD

SHE'S ALL I EVER HAD

Words and Music by
ROBI ROSA, GEORGE NORIEGA
and JON SECADA

She's All I Ever Had - 2 - 1
IF9939

SMOOTH

Lyrics by
ROB THOMAS

Music by
ITAAL SHUR and ROB THOMAS

Moderate latin rock

Smooth - 2 - 1
IF9939

SOMEDAY

Words and Music by
SUGAR RAY and DAVID KAHNE

Someday - 2 - 1
IF9939